I0091296

This manual has questions designed to be used in leading classroom discussion. The questions are of three types:

The ***first*** *type of questions check that the material has been read and understood.*

The ***second*** *group of questions is to check more than just comprehension of the material. They check if the student is capable of applying what he or she has learned.*

The ***third*** *set of questions are open ended. The author does not necessarily know the answers to them either. These are questions intended to push the envelope of our understanding of the concepts. The questions should lead to debate, and it is expected that some debates will end inconclusively. It is not the answer that counts but the quality of the discussion.*

I invite those teaching the material to send me new questions, doubts, and disagreements about the material that arise as they go about teaching it.Please send me cases, stories, examples, and even cartoons that pertain to this material. Doing so will improve the next edition of the book.

I truly thank you in advance for your willingness.

Sincerely,
Ichak Kalderon Adizes

-Conversation 1-

Comprehension Questions

1 What is the translation, if any, of the word "management" in any language you know?

2 What does "to manage" mean to you?

3 What do *you* consider to be the difference between management and leadership?

4 Discuss why making decisions in conditions of change means decision making under uncertainty.

5 Discuss why implementation and risk are related.

6 Give an example in which a solution to problem A created problem B, which was worse than problem A.

7 Discuss a situation where a change in one area had a domino effect, impacting multiple other areas.

8 Give an example from your experience that manifests the statement "If there is

no change the mediocre eventually catch up."

9 Give an example of an effective decision you made that was badly implemented, and why.

10 Give an example of a bad decision you have made that was well implemented and why.

Application Questions

1 The higher the rate of change the higher the rates of divorce and crime rate. Do you agree? Explain your answer.

2 Can you give examples that show that the managerial or leadership process is not value-free, that it has political underpinnings?

3 Do you have an example in which motivation was a manipulation?

4 Give an example where change caused problems.

5 Can you give examples where the standard of living has gone up but *caused* a reduction in quality of life?

6 Give an example from personal life, business, or society where a problem was an opportunity in disguise.

7 Give examples from the following realms in which change was the cause of problems: mechanical, social, psychological, and political.

Development Questions

1 When we die does change stop?

2 Does change really ever stop?

3 What is the difference between change while alive and change while dead?

4 Is change always destructive?

5 Is human intervention in nature constructive or destructive?

6 What is easier: to destroy or to build? Why?

7 What is easier to hate or to love? Why?

8 Can diseases that have mutated from animals to humans—such as AIDS—be attributed to change? How?

9 Will the next big war humans have be against microbes or viruses that are immune to medicine? Why?

-Conversation 2-

Review Questions

1 "People are scared to make a decision because it involves risk." Do you think this statement is true or false? Discuss.

2 "When there is change, there is no way to avoid deciding and implementing." True or false? Discuss.

3 "There wouldn't be a need for government if there weren't change." Do you agree? Explain your point of view.

4 "There would be no need for parenting if there were no change." Do you agree?

5 Think of a case where not deciding was deciding.

6 Think of a decision you have made and planned the implementation in detail, but that did not work out as planned. What happened?

7 Give an example from business or political science in which efforts for internal integration caused external disintegration, and where efforts on external integration caused internal disintegration.

8 Do you have an example of a leader who has done external and internal integration successfully? Describe, analyze, and share.

9 Explain why a stair function of revenues, or of profits, is good, and better than straight up curve.

10 Find an example of a business leader or political leader who has successfully changed his or her style as the system he or she was leading was changing.

11 "Conflict is necessary and indispensable for good management, good governing of a country, and, come to think of it, for a marriage too." Does this make sense to you? Why or why not?

Application Questions

1 If the way to heal is to integrate, does aliphatic medicine heal? What does heal?

2 Discuss a case from history in which a leader's decision was not implemented. Why?

3 Discuss a disastrous decision that was made by a dictator and was swiftly implemented.

4 President Obama has pushed through decisions by executive order and has been accused of undermining the democratic process. Use the Adizes concepts to explain what happened.

5 "Totalitarian regimes are efficient but ineffective." Give some examples from history that illustrate this statement.

6 "People usually prefer *more* to *instead of*. Give examples of this from personal life.

7 "To heal is to integrate." Do you agree? Give examples from mechanical engineering, political science, and business life.

8 Discuss an example of a decision made in a democratic society that had major difficulties being implemented. What happened?

9 Identify a problem you are struggling with now. What has “fallen apart?” What has changed?

10 How does Schumpeter’s theory of constructive revolution fit with the Adizes theory?

11 How does the role of the God Shiva in the Hindu religion correspond to the Adizes theory?

12 Find an example of a company or country that has grown fast and disintegrated because of it.

13 Describe a problem that was an opportunity, and an opportunity that was a problem.

14 Describe a marriage you know of that is a complementary team.

15 Does your company have meetings for strategic decision making separate from operational meetings? How differently are they being conducted?

16 Does your family have routine strategic or operational meetings? Are the meetings successful?

17 Can you think of some cases in which there was management of change and there was no conflict? Was it successful? Why?

18 Think of a case from personal life or political science in which the more change there was the more conflict there was.

19 Have you ever avoided conflict by avoiding change? What happened? Were you happy?

Development Questions

1 If integration is the solution to problems caused by change, is democracy, which legitimizes dissention, functional in times of chronic, rapid change?

2 People who meditate, do yoga, and accept life as is, live in the present and appear to have no problems. Yet Adizes theory says people have no problems only when they are dead. Who is right or wrong?

3 Dictatorship looks as if it integrates. Brings peace. So, is a dictatorship the solution to countries with rapid change?

-Conversation 3-

Review Questions

1 What would four people with **(P)** styles claim is the problem and solution when diagnosing a situation?

2 What would four **(A)** styles claim is the solution to a problem?

3 What would four **(E)** styles claim is the problem, and what would their solution be?

4 What would the solution be if there were a complementary team, but no **(I)**?

5 Morale is low. Which role is missing?

6 Too much **(E)** will cause which other role(s) to suffer?

7 Too much **(A)** will cause which other role(s) to suffer?

8 Could too much **(I)** be undesirable? Why or why not?

9 "The **(P)** role enables the organization to satisfy its customers' needs." True or false?

10 "Good **(P)** managers must be knowledgeable of their profession." Do you agree or disagree?

11 Good **(P)** managers must be achievement oriented. Do you agree?

Application Questions

1 What is the difference between Adizes interventions and McKinsey consulting? BCG consulting? Steven Covey training?

2 Think of a recent decision you have made. What need was it supposed to satisfy? Are you always aware of the need your decisions are supposedly satisfying?

3 Do you know of a company that is so preoccupied with profits that it is going bankrupt? How did that happen? Did it happen right away or over time? Why?

4 Give some examples where focusing on the *how* is more important than focusing on the *what*.

5 In your personal life which values are not negotiable (i.e., you will not violate them)?

6 In choosing a partner/spouse, did values play a role in making your decision? What was the driving factor?

7 Think of a situation where you focused more on the goal than on the means of reaching the goal. What happened?

8 Do you have an example in which workers have made a company shine, and an example where workers can make a company fail miserably in the marketplace?

9 Think of a government that does not serve its people, but only serves itself.

10 What is the purpose of your organization?

11 Articulate the difference between customers and clients.

12 A family is going for breakfast at McDonalds. Who is the client? Who is the customer?

13 Who are the clients of an organization's quality assurance and control department?

14 Who are the clients of an audit department in an organization?

15 In which kind of company are investors the clients?

16 Are stockholders the reason why a business organization *was* established?

17 Is profit the goal of a commercial entity? Will not a company that is for profit suffer if it does not focus on profits?

18 What is the goal of a philanthropic organization?

19 Think of constraint goals for a sales organization.

Development Questions

1 When will the means justify the goal?

2 Do you agree with the statement "every worker should be a manager and every manager a worker?"

3 Who is the client of a prison? Who is the customer?

4 Who is the client of a high school? Who is the customer?

5 Who is the client of a police force? Who is the customer?

6 Who is the client of a single artist—say, a painter or a musician? Who is the customer?

7 For what do *you* exist?

8 How do you measure the effectiveness of a theater?

9 How do you measure the effectiveness of a country?

10 How do you measure the effectiveness of a marriage?

-Conversation 4-

Review Questions

1 Doing the right thing is which role?

2 Doing it right is which role?

3 Describe a company in which efficiency undermined effectiveness.

4 Describe a situation in which effectiveness undermined efficiency.

5 Why would chronic and rapid change cause bureaucracy?

6 Is it always true that it is better to be approximately right than precisely wrong?

7 Why are profits a measurement of added value?

8 Why does satisfying long-term client needs produce long-term effectiveness?

9 How does being proactive make a company effective in the long term?

10 Does all planning make an organization proactive?

11 "Create your future today." How is this done?

12 When will the right strategy be to change slowly in order not to die quickly?

13 Why must an entrepreneur have **(P)**?

14 "An entrepreneur must be achievement oriented." Do you agree or not?

15 Why is integration an active verb? Why can it not be a passive verb?

16 Does a housewife have all those she needs to dispense her responsibility reporting to her?

17 Who are the "clients" of your heart? Of the rectum?

18 "Leaders should never admit a weakness." Is that true or false?

19 Think of those whom you need in your job but do not pay with money. How do you "pay" them?

20 When you cooperate without expecting a reward, why do you do it?

21 How do you reward those working for you? Only with money?

22 When a company's departments behave like silos, what is missing?

23 Describe a company in which management is considered "outsiders." Why are they outsiders?

24 Describe a country where government is considered "outsiders." Why?

25 Which country is high in **(I)**? Which in **(A)**, which in **(E)**, and which in **(P)**?

26 Why is fusion not desirable, though integration is?

27 The efforts to bring peace in the Middle East are done via external intervention and mediation. Are the relations between Israel and the Palestinians organic or mechanistic?

28 If there is mutual trust and respect in the Middle East, will the relationship be organic or mechanistic?

29 What kind of a strategy is an **(E)** strategy? How about a **(P)** strategy?

30 Describe an **(I)** or **(A)** strategy.

31 Explain why **(I)** is indispensable.

32 Why is a **(PaE-)** person not an entrepreneur?

33 "To love is more difficult than to hate." Do you agree? Why or why not?

Application Questions

1 Describe how cutting costs to increase profits in the short term can cause a loss of profits in the long term.

2 Will finding new clients in the future qualify a company as being effective in the long term?

3 What is your "rock?"

4 Will being proactive always work in changing the company at the speed of the changing environment?

5 What does it mean that a company should position itself in order to be proactive?

6 Discuss: "One honeymoon is not enough for a lifetime of a marriage" using Adizes theory.

7 What is the purpose of a marriage? *Is, want, and should.*

8 What is the purpose of a city? *Is, want, and should.*

9 What is the purpose of a country? *Is, want, or should.*

10 If you are in a romantic relationship, what is the purpose of that relationship? If it is working, why is it working? If not, why not?

Development Questions

1 Developmental psychology claims that the purpose of human beings is to reproduce. How does that fit with Adizes theory?

2 Would economists agree that profits are not a deterministic goal but a constraint goal? What happens to economic theory if profits are accepted as a constraint goal?

3 "Change fast or die slowly" is not always right. You might die quickly too. Discuss when that will happen.

4 Sociological theory claims that the goal of an organization is to survive. How does that fit with Adizes theory?

5 What is the **(P)** of a social entrepreneur? Is there such an entity?

6 Does political entrepreneurship exist? If so, what is its **(P)**?

7 Must an artist be achievement oriented? If he or she is, what kind of an artist will that be?

8 What is the **(P)** of a pure artist?

9 What is the **(P)** of a politician?

10 Why, as organizations age, do they lose sight of who their clients are?

11 Is it true that the more developed a nation is the more disempowered its people will feel? Why or why not?

12 If you exist for yourself, you are a cancer. Then are all pure artists cancerous?

13 Only if you believe that pure art (art for the sake of self-expression) serves no purpose in society. For whom do non-commercial artists exist?

14 To whom do you think a Dalai Lama feels responsible?

15 What is the **(P)** of a wife? A husband?

16 What is the **(P)** of a mother? Father?

17 Could there be a conflict between being a mother and a wife?

18 Could there be a conflict between being a father and a husband?

19 What is the purpose of a marriage? What should it be? What do you want it to be?

20 What is the purpose of a city? In *is*, *want*, and *should* terms.

21 What is the purpose of a country? *Is*, *want*, and *should*.

22 "**(I)** is forever." What does that mean?

23 How would you combat those who do not accept differentiation?

24 Which system has better chance to survive in the long term: those that are totalitarian or those that are democratic? Why?

25 "An organization as a form of functional interdependence is born in the way a body as an embodiment of the spirit is born." Do you agree? Explain.

-Conversation 5-

Review Questions

1 Think of a situation you have had in which time pressure undermined teamwork.

2 Identify a case where too much change undermined effectiveness and short-term results.

3 Find a case from your personal experience in which the **(P)** and **(E)** roles were in conflict. Discuss.

4 Entrepreneurs want stable environment to invest. Why?

5 Discuss a case from history in which **(E)**s were persecuted by **(A)**s.

6 How did you fall in love, in an **(I)**, **(P)**, or **(E)** environment?

7 When have you experienced **(I)**? Describe and analyze what happened in (PAEI) terms.

8 "Crime is an **(I)** deficiency problem." Do you agree? If so, how would you treat it?

9 Can you find evidence that the higher the rate of change, the higher the divorce rate? Explain the phenomena.

10 What is the **(PAEI)** code for quality assurance? For quality control?

Application Questions

1 Analyze the history of a religion and determine whether it followed the progression from **(I)** to **(A)**.

2 Think of a problem you are having right now. What caused it? What changed?

3 What would be the **(PAEI)** solutions to your problem?

4 Who are your clients now?

5 Who are the clients of a car manufacturing company? Who are the customers?

6 Evaluate the education system in your country. Is it creating an environment in which students want to learn and learn

how to learn, or is it mostly teaching students to know?

7 Discuss why disruptive, chronic change generates corruption.

8 What is music in **(PAEI)** code?

9 Is the processed food industry a curse or blessing? Why?

10 How would you train managers to open their hearts more?

Development Questions

1 Do you agree that one grows by taking responsibility? Deliberate.

2 "Creative people make a mess but want order." Do you agree? Discuss why or why not.

3 "Only a strong authoritarian leader can bring democracy in a culture that has never experienced it." Do you agree? Discuss.

-Conversation 6-

Review Questions

1 Exercise for estimating (PAEI) style: This section includes descriptive excerpts about five well-known individuals. You are to come up with an overall **(PAEI)** style rating for each person using a scale of **-5 to +5**, rate:

- each style
- on each role
- on each line

Using the above scale, write down your rating for each role on each line. Indicate, in your judgment, if one or more of the four roles is performed or deficient.

When you are finished, add all the points and see whether the overall ranking of the style of the individual reflects your general impression.

(I) ALAN LADD, JR. - Excerpt from "In the Office of Alan Ladd, Jr." *Esquire Magazine*, April 02, 1978.

The **first** thing that people say about Alan Ladd, Jr. is that he is a good listener.

The **second** thing they say about him is that he makes money. In 1976 he became president of Twentieth Century Fox and soon turned the studio around. This year he has "STAR WARS," the highest grossing movie in the motion picture industry, which he picked up after both Universal and United Artists passed it up. Amazingly, he picked up "STAR WARS" on the basis of twelve pages of script.

The **third** thing people say about Ladd is that they can't figure out how he does it. He certainly doesn't talk about it.

The first thing Ladd does when he reaches his office is study the overnight sales figures on his movies and on the competition. The gross sheets serve as a basis for strategy. "We use them," he says, "to make a decision on whether to keep spending on the advertising. If the picture isn't doing well, then maybe we should come up with a gimmick of some kind." Ladd continues, "You always have to keep changing in this business—attitudes, methods, everything." There seems to be a bit of irony to his statement as Ladd is a man who likes organization and planning.

Ladd's instinct to go with the filmmakers is perhaps the real key to his success. Unlike other studio heads, he has no ambition to direct a movie and therefore is not in conflict, real, imagined, or potential, with anyone he hires. An unusual situation in the film business, he trusts the filmmakers and they trust him. Says Mel Brooks, "You wanna know the secret to Laddie's success? He leaves you alone."

That is not completely true, however, as Ladd maintains tight financial control. A filmmaker must deal with him concerning every penny in the production's budget.

But to understand what Mel Brooks and others mean by Ladd's hands- off policy, you must consider what Fox was like under Ladd's most famous predecessor, Darryl F. Zanuck. Zanuck was personally involved in every foot of film that came out of his studio. Not just in the conception and casting but in the writing, the building of sets, the shooting, editing, the cutting and the distribution. If he awoke one night with an idea, he would order up a script. He worked closely with the writers, personally going over each line. He rewrote. He polished. He hovered over directors on the sets. He edited. He re-edited. And when the shooting was done, he cut and then re-cut. At production meeting he would pace around the room swinging his polo mallet. He would scream. He would gesticulate wildly, constantly puffing on his cigar. He would rip into scripts, reject ideas, act out parts. Compared to that, Ladd leaves people alone.

P

A

E

I

Impressions

____

____

____

(II) **HOWARD HEAD** - Excerpt from "Howard Head Changed Winter with His Metal Ski; Now His Prince Shakes Up Tennis," *People Weekly*, April 18, 1977

In 1950 Howard Head perfected the first metal skis, which were quickly dismissed as a gimmick. But the skis turned out to be more responsive and stronger than the conventional hickory ones and Head soon became the leading manufacturer of metal skis. In 1971, AMF, Inc. bought the company and "Head" now appears on sporting goods from conventional tennis rackets to bathing suits.

In 1976 the Prince racket, which Head claims has "the shape a racket should have in the first place," hit the market. More than 100,000 rackets were sold in the first year, signaling the same success for the Prince racket as for the metal skis. "I have no doubt," says Head, "that in three or four years this will be the conventional racket and the others will be thought of as old fashioned."

What has been the secret behind Head's success as an innovator? Says friend Thomas J. Watson, Jr., retired chairman of IBM, "The visionary engineer who's just a nice guy never gets his product on the market. Howard is both visionary and hard-minded."

Daughter Nancy has another answer: "If he gets annoyed with something, he changes it." Adds his wife, "Howard never gives up."

Head responds to these assessments with, "That's true." Furthermore, he says, never letting false modesty cloud his vision, "The idea for an invention is only five percent. Making it practical is 95 percent of the job. You have to have a perfectionist streak, and you have to let that streak run until the product works."

His interest in skiing began in 1947. The lanky aviation engineer found that he was barely able to make a snowplow turn and finally a reasoned that "If hickory was the best material for skis, then they'd make airplanes out of it, too." He bought some scrap aluminum and after several years of trial and error, he had perfected the metal ski. "If I had known then that it would take 40 versions before the ski was any good, I might have given up. But fortunately, you get trapped into thinking the next design will be it."

Even after his company became financially successful, Head attended to the most minute detail. Early Head skis actually bear serial numbers inscribed by Head himself. But as the company began suffering growing pains and moved from $10 to $20 million in annual sales, the company began to suffer. "I was a very inept manager," Head concedes. "I compulsively had to do everything. Whenever I was dissatisfied, instead of taking it up with whoever had done it and getting them to do it better, I would just do it myself. That's when I ran out of gas, and the company began to suffer."

Head's personal life also took a series of downhill spills. His first marriage ended after six years and his daughter moved with her mother to South Carolina. "Shortly thereafter," Head recalls, "I got so immersed in the ski project that I just didn't have the emotional energy to pay attention to my own daughter. I didn't begin to know Nancy until she was about 12."

Another marriage, in 1960, broke up in just three years. "I was really married to skiing all that time," Head explains. "I like to think that since my divorce from Head I have devoted myself to a successful job of marriage to Joan and to learning how to have more fun and satisfaction with people in general."

Today, Head is the unsalaried chairman of the Prince board and a major stockholder. Asked about using technology to perfect the tools of sport, Head replies, "If a racket had a built-in computer that would always hit the ball for you, it would be destructive. If you could build a ski with an automatic stabilizing device, that would be destructive. I think my ski and my racket make both sports more pleasurable and accessible."

P

A

E

I

Impressions

(III) CALVIN COOLIDGE - Excerpt from James O. Sarber, "Classifying and Predicting Presidential Style." 1968

Calvin Coolidge's strength was not effort but patience. "Let well enough alone" was his motto. He kept Harding's cabinet, let Daugherty hang on for a long time and tried to delay the efforts of his friends who wanted to support him in 1924. Asked how he kept fit, he replied, "By avoiding the big problems."

Coolidge got rid of much work by giving it to others and he believed in doing just that. As he would say, "One rule of action more important than all others consists in never doing anything that someone else can do for you." He appointed or retained those men who had sufficient ability to solve all the problems that came under their jurisdiction. He rarely interfered and he resented others who interfered with him.

Coolidge was always surrounded by people. Alone, he said, he got "a sort of naked feeling." Yet, his poker face and long impenetrable silences gave rise to scores of anecdotes. Generally, he would just sit. As he would say, "Can't hang you for what you don't say."

He did not particularly enjoy being President, given all the demands that were placed upon him and he conserved his energies stingily. He concentrated on matters only the President had to decide and defined that category as narrowly as possible. Most everything could wait.

And Coolidge himself could wait, with utter, unflappable calm for longer than the last of his advisors. He also managed to rationalize his independence of others: Clearly his style in close interpersonal relations cut him off effectively from much of Washington controversy and also from any effective political bargaining with administrative or legislative or party leaders. He was a loner who endured in order to serve, while the nation drifted.

P

A

E

I

Impressions

(IV) **CYRUS R. VANCE** - Excerpt from: "Man at Helm: Skillful but No Innovator," *U.S. News & World Report*, January 23, 1978.

Cyrus R. Vance is unpretentious to the point of shyness, tireless—he works an average of 14 hours a day—and seemingly has no enemies. He shuns publicity and in official meetings often takes his own notes. Although he holds one of the most critical positions in the Carter Administration, few Americans know him.

He is described by his peers and subordinates as decent, courageous, decisive, an excellent trouble-shooter and executor of policy. But he is not looked upon as a creative policy innovator or a strategic planner capable of orchestrating a complex array of international initiatives.

He is low-keyed and non-combative but still no "yes man." Friends recall how, early in 1968, he rattled President Johnson by advising disengagement in Vietnam. Although he had strongly supported the war, in the earlier stages, he had at this time decided that the cost of the war in terms of domestic dissension and disorder had made it prohibitive.

Those inside the State Department give his performance mixed reviews. On the one hand, many feel that he-has restored initiative and made many people feel more productive. As one official put it, "Vance, unlike Kissinger, is open and wants his aides to participate actively in the affairs of the department."

Others see Vance as a no-nonsense guy. He listens patiently to others without revealing his own feelings. When all is said and done, though, he makes a decision and expects no back talk.

A retired Foreign Service officer sees Vance as a skillful lawyer, excellent at grasping and arguing a brief. "But he does not conceptualize or provide a framework or priorities for foreign policy. He takes on each issue as his client, the President, sends it along. What's missing at the State Department under Vance is the art of diplomacy, the art of statecraft."

Unlike his predecessor Henry Kissinger, when Vance travels abroad he delegates authority to his subordinates in Washington to make all but the most important decisions.

Again, unlike Kissinger, he has, as one diplomatic correspondent said, "demonstrated that he can easily survive not talking to newsmen."

In most countries Vance is viewed as a messenger and salesman rather than as a shaper of U.S. foreign policy. In London, one rare editorial about the Secretary describes him a "worthy but low-key operator."

In Germany officials see Vance as reliable and trustworthy yet unimpressive and ever hapless during his first year in office.
To the Asians, Vance appears as a salesman promoting a product that he had only a minor role in designing. And to the Russians, Vance seems the mystery man of the Administration (not a single major article has appeared on Vance in the controlled Soviet press.)

In the Middle East, the Arabs and Israel alike seem to welcome and appreciate his talents. According to the *U.S. News & World Report* bureau in the area: "Vance fills the bill for what people in the Mideast want now—a low key individual who shuns diplomatic theatrics and can be trusted in a way that his predecessor was not."

In Washington, the President seems to be looking increasingly to Vance as an invaluable and trusted representative responsible for implementing and selling U.S. foreign policy at home and abroad.

P

A

E

I

Impressions

(V) PETER GRACE, JR. - Excerpt from a profile in *Fortune Magazine*, May 1978.

During his busy thirty-three years at the helm of W. R. Grace & Co. J. Peter Grace Jr. completely transformed the company created by his forebears. Not a single business survives from the day Peter took over in place of the old W. R. Grace & Co. there is another much bigger company with the same name.

The transformation of the company has not been without extraordinary turmoil. The company purchased about 130 businesses in the last thirty years and just since 1960 has unloaded about sixty. And today the company is still in flux.

W. R. Grace reflects the extraordinary personality of the man who heads it. Beyond the mere effects of longevity and family connection, there is an even stronger linkage between Peter and his company— the sheer force of his personality, imposing on W. R. Grace his own tremendous drive and energy.

From the beginning, Peter looked upon "saving" the company as a kind of crusade. He is fiercely competitive, determined to succeed in everything he does. He candidly admits that "there is nothing I dislike more than being a loser in anything."

Obsessed with time, he claims he does not waste a minute. On the way to and from his office he dictates to one of his seven secretaries or talks on one or both of his car's telephones. After dinner he puts in another four hours poring over papers.

All this leaves little time for diversions. "Who says you need kicks," he replies.

To maintain a firm grip on his company's numerous operating units, Peter relies on a fantastic profusion of numbers. “The numbers are the facts,” he says. “Numbers are reality.”

The passion for numbers is indulged by the “spreadsheet,” a huge mass of figures neatly laid out in columns. “I look at everything on a spreadsheet basis,” he says. One departed executive remembers compiling a spreadsheet with 1,000 columns for a $2 million expenditure. When fully extended is stretched for sixty feet. And of the approximately 300 charts that one group prepared last year, ten were actually presented. The rest were prepared in case Peter asked about a particular subject.

With all of his dependence on numbers, he is capable of impulsive behavior. One morning in 1968, he stopped for breakfast at a Phoenix restaurant which was a member of a restaurant chain. “It was the best breakfast since my mother’s buckwheat cakes,” he recalls. By the next morning, he was in Newport Beach, California, to discuss buying the whole chain. Two years later, he did buy it and today it forms the backbone of Grace’s restaurant operations.

One long-time advisor noted that "Peter's basic philosophy is that scale is an important aspect of profitability." Scale was also an important measure of security. Bigness, for Peter, would ensure the future viability of the company.

A search for a new direction and new acquisitions outside the field of chemicals (Grace is the nation's fifth biggest producer of chemicals) began in earnest in the early 1960s. Peter dreamed of building a General Foods of Europe and bought producers of chocolate in the Netherlands, ice cream in Denmark and Italy, chewing gum in Germany and others.

The strategy, however, was poorly conceived, and the construction of a large food distribution system never worked in practice. For one thing, Grace discovered that ingrained national tastes were not transportable. For another thing, the implementation was faulty. As Grace's chief financial officer said, "We were acquiring second-rate businesses." In addition, Grace never found the right managers to take over. "The whole damn thing was management," Peter lamented. "You could have built ice cream, you could have built yogurt, you could have had all kinds of products and a huge distribution system...if you had the right people."

Measured against the objective of corporate security, Peter Grace's stewardship of the company has certainly been a success. And he goes so far as to say, "I think I've done a fair job living up to my obligations."

The complexity of the company Peter Grace built is extensive, and a state of flux is a normality. As long as Peter Grace is in charge, one thing is sure: W. R. Grace will be buying companies in the future—and selling companies, too.

P

A

E

I

____

____

Impressions

____

____

____

2 The following is the inaugural address given by President Barack Obama in, 2009. From this speech, how would analyze Obama's style? How would you predict he would conduct foreign policy?

"My fellow citizens:

I stand here today humbled by the task before us, grateful for the trust you have bestowed, mindful of the sacrifices borne by our ancestors. I thank President Bush for his service to our nation, as well as the generosity and cooperation he has shown throughout this transition. Forty-four Americans have now taken the presidential oath.[1] The words have been spoken during rising tides of prosperity and the still waters of peace. Yet, every so often the oath is taken amidst gathering clouds and raging storms. At these moments, America has carried on not simply because of the skill or vision of those in high office, but because We the People have remained faithful to the ideals of our forbearers, and true to our founding documents.

So, it has been. So, it must be with this generation of Americans. That we are in the midst of crisis is now well understood. Our nation is at war, against a far-reaching network of violence and hatred. Our economy is badly weakened, a consequence of greed and irresponsibility on the part of some, but also our collective failure to make hard choices and prepare the nation for a new age. Homes have been lost; jobs shed; businesses shuttered. Our health care is too costly; our schools fail too many; and each day brings further evidence that the ways we use energy strengthen our adversaries and threaten our planet.

These are the indicators of crisis, subject to data and statistics. Less measurable but no less profound is a sapping of confidence across our land — a nagging fear that America's decline is inevitable, and that the next generation must lower its sights.

Today I say to you that the challenges we face are real. They are serious and they are many. They will not be met easily or in a short span of time. But know this, America — they will be met. On this day, we gather because we have chosen hope over fear, unity of purpose over conflict and discord. On this day, we come to proclaim an end to the petty grievances and false promises, the recriminations and worn- out dogmas, that for far too long have strangled our politics. We remain a young nation, but in the words of Scripture, the time has come to set aside childish things. The time has come to reaffirm our enduring spirit; to choose our better history; to carry forward that precious gift, that noble idea, passed on from generation to generation: the God-given promise that all are equal, all are free, and all deserve a chance to pursue their full measure of happiness. In reaffirming the greatness of our nation, we understand that greatness is never a given. It must be earned. Our journey has never been one of short-cuts or settling-for-less. It has not been the path for the faint-hearted — for those who prefer leisure over work, or seek only the pleasures of riches and fame. Rather, it has been the risk- takers, the doers, the makers of things — some celebrated but more often men and women obscure in their labor, who have carried us up the long, rugged path towards prosperity and freedom.

For us, they packed up their few worldly possessions and traveled across oceans in search of a new life. For us, they toiled in sweatshops and settled the West; endured the lash of the whip and plowed the hard earth.

For us, they fought and died, in places like Concord and Gettysburg; Normandy and

Khe Sanh. Time and again these men and women struggled and sacrificed and worked till their hands were raw so that we might live a better life. They saw America as bigger than the sum of our individual ambitions; greater than all the differences of birth or wealth or faction.

This is the journey we continue today. We remain the most prosperous, powerful nation on Earth. Our workers are no less productive than when this crisis began. Our minds are no less inventive, our goods and services no less needed than they were last week or last month or last year. Our capacity remains undiminished. But our time of standing pat, of protecting narrow interests and putting off unpleasant decisions — that time has surely passed. Starting today, we must pick ourselves up, dust ourselves off, and begin again the work of remaking America.

For everywhere we look, there is work to be done. The state of the economy calls for action, bold and swift, and we will act — not only to create new jobs, but to lay a new foundation for growth. We will build the roads and bridges, the electric grids and digital lines that feed our commerce and bind us together. We will restore science to its rightful place, and wield technology's wonders to raise health care's quality and lower its cost. We will harness the sun and the winds and the soil to fuel our cars and run our factories. And we will transform our schools and colleges and universities to meet the demands of a new age. All this we can do. All this we will do.

Now, there are some who question the scale of our ambitions — who suggest that our system cannot tolerate too many big plans. Their memories are short. For they have forgotten what this country has already done; what free men and women can achieve when imagination is joined to common purpose, and necessity to courage. What the cynics fail to understand is that the ground has shifted beneath them — that the stale political arguments that have consumed us for so long no longer apply. The question we ask today is not whether our government is too big or too small, but whether it works — whether it helps families find jobs at a decent wage, care they can afford, a retirement that is dignified. Where the answer is yes, we intend to move forward. Where the answer is no, programs will end. And those of us who manage the public's dollars will be held to account — to spend wisely, reform bad habits, and do our business in the light of day — because only then can we restore the vital trust between a people and their government.

Nor is the question before us whether the market is a force for good or ill. Its power to generate wealth and expand freedom is unmatched, but this crisis has reminded us that without a watchful eye, the market can spin out of control — and that a nation cannot prosper long when it favors only the prosperous. The success of our economy has always depended not just on the size of our Gross Domestic Product, but on the reach of our prosperity; on our ability to extend opportunity to every willing heart — not out of charity, but because it is the surest route to our common good.

As for our common defense, we reject as false the choice between our safety and our ideals. Our Founding Fathers, faced with perils we can scarcely imagine, drafted a charter to assure the rule of law and the rights of man, a charter expanded by the blood of generations. Those ideals still light the world, and we will not give them up for expediency's sake. And so to all the other peoples and governments who are watching today, from the grandest capitals to the small village where my father was born: know that America is a friend of each nation and every man, woman, and child who seeks a future of peace and dignity, and that we are ready to lead once more. Recall that earlier generations faced down fascism and communism not just with missiles and tanks, but with sturdy alliances and enduring convictions. They understood that our power alone cannot protect us, nor does it entitle us to do as we please. Instead, they knew that our power grows through its prudent use; our security emanates from the justness of our cause, the force of our example, the tempering qualities of humility and restraint.

We are the keepers of this legacy. Guided by these principles once more, we can meet those new threats that demand even greater effort — even greater cooperation and understanding between nations. We will begin to responsibly leave Iraq to its people and forge a hard- earned peace in Afghanistan. With old friends and former foes, we will work tirelessly to lessen the nuclear threat, and roll back the specter of a warming planet. We will not apologize for our way of life, nor will we waver in its defense, and for those who seek to advance their aims by inducing terror and slaughtering innocents, we say to you now that our spirit is stronger and cannot be broken; you cannot outlast us, and we will defeat you.

For we know that our patchwork heritage is a strength, not a weakness. We are a nation of Christians and Muslims, Jews and Hindus — and non-believers. We are shaped by every language and culture, drawn from every end of this Earth; and because we have tasted the bitter swill of civil war and segregation, and emerged from that dark chapter stronger and more united, we cannot help but believe that the old hatreds shall someday pass; that the lines of tribe shall soon dissolve; that as the world grows smaller, our common humanity shall reveal itself; and that America must play its role in ushering in a new era of peace.

To the Muslim world, we seek a new way forward, based on mutual interest and mutual respect.

To those leaders around the globe who seek to sow conflict or blame their society's ills on the West — know that your people will judge you on what you can build, not what you destroy. To those who cling to power through corruption and deceit and the silencing of dissent, know that you are on the wrong side of history; but that we will extend a hand if you are willing to unclench your fist.

To the people of poor nations, we pledge to work alongside you to make your farms flourish and let clean waters flow; to nourish starved bodies and feed hungry minds. And to those nations like ours that enjoy relative plenty, we say we can no longer afford indifference to the suffering outside our borders; nor can we consume the world's resources without regard to the effect. For the world has changed, and we must change with it.

As we consider the road that unfolds before us, we remember with humble gratitude those brave Americans who, at this very hour, patrol far-off deserts and distant mountains. They have something to tell us, just as the fallen heroes who lie in Arlington whisper through the ages.

We honor them not only because they are guardians of our liberty, but because they embody the spirit of service; a willingness to find meaning in something greater than themselves. And yet, at this moment — a moment that will define a generation — it is precisely this spirit that must inhabit us all.

For as much as government can do and must do, it is ultimately the faith and determination of the American people upon which this nation relies. It is the kindness to take in a stranger when the levees break, the selflessness of workers who would rather cut their hours than see a friend lose their job which sees us through our darkest hours. It is the firefighter's courage to storm a stairway filled with smoke, but also a parent's willingness to nurture a child, that finally decides our fate.

Our challenges may be new. The instruments with which we meet them may be new. But those values upon which our success depends — honesty and hard work, courage and fair play, tolerance and curiosity, loyalty and patriotism — these things are old. These things are true. They have been the quiet force of progress throughout our history. What is demanded then is a return to these truths. What is required of us now is a new era of responsibility — a recognition, on the part of every American, that we have duties to ourselves, our nation, and the world — duties that we do not grudgingly accept but rather seize gladly, firm in the knowledge that there is nothing so satisfying to the spirit, so defining of our character, than giving our all to a difficult task.

This is the price and the promise of citizenship.

This is the source of our confidence — the knowledge that God calls on us to shape an uncertain destiny.

This is the meaning of our liberty and our creed — why men and women and children of every race and every faith can join in celebration across this magnificent mall, and why a man whose father less than sixty years ago might not have been served at a local restaurant can now stand before you to take a most sacred oath.

So, let us mark this day with remembrance, of who we are and how far we have traveled. In the year of America's birth, in the coldest of months, a small band of patriots huddled by dying campfires on the shores of an icy river. The capital was abandoned. The enemy was advancing. The snow was stained with blood. At a moment when the outcome of our revolution was most in doubt, the father of our nation ordered these words be read to the people:[2]

"Let it be told to the future world...that in the depth of winter, when nothing but hope and virtue could survive...that the city and the country, alarmed at one common danger, came forth to meet [it]."[3] America, in the face of our common dangers, in this winter of our hardship, let us remember these timeless words. With hope and virtue, let us brave once more the icy currents, and endure what storms may come. Let it be said by our children's children that when we were tested we refused to let this journey end, that we did not turn back nor did we falter; and with eyes fixed on the horizon and God's grace upon us, we carried forth that great gift of freedom and delivered it safely to future generations.

Thank you. God bless you. And God bless the United States of America."

3 Analyze the personality style of a character in a book you have read and classify it in **(PAEI)** terms.

4 What will a person with a Lone Ranger style do if, for some reason, they have nothing to do?

5 What name do people give to the Lone Ranger style in your city, industry, or language?

6 How does the **(P---)** style train people?

7 Who suffers from a managerial disease called "manualitis?"

8 Who confuses form with function?

9 Which style is precisely wrong, and which style is precisely right all the time?

10 Which style is seldom right but never in doubt?

11 Who complains most that he or she is not well understood?

12 Which style has a propensity to be maniac depressive?

13 Which style hedges a lot?

Application Questions

1 Does a person's style change? Ever or over time? With experience? Do people change at all?

2 Why don't you know your style as well as you know other people's styles?

3 Which style complains that people are not committed enough?

4 Which style's subordinates usually do not know what the mission of the organization is or what the priorities they have to follow are?

5 What should be the style of a sales manager?

6 What should be the style of a financial analyst?

7 What should be the style of a stockbroker?

Development Questions

1 How would you change a **(P---)** style or an **(-A--)** style?

2 Can you change an **(--E-)** style?

3 Which style is easier to change, **(P)** or **(I)**?

4 How would you go about developing **(P)** capabilities?

5 **(A)** capabilities?

6 **(E)** capabilities?

7 **(I)** capabilities?

8 Why must a leader have **(I)** capabilities? What if she has only **(I)**?

9 Do you know your own style?

10 Which style has the most difficulty motivating people; which style over expects?

11 Why is it that the more you try to control the more you need to control?

12 "If you lie low and do not make waves for long enough, you might get promoted, maybe even to the role of president a bureaucratic company." Is this true or false? Why?

13 Which style has a scapegoat of the day, as if he must always accuse someone else of being responsible for failures?

14 What should be the style of a financial assets manager?

Development Questions

1 Discuss the following statement: We are different and, at the same time, similar.

2 Who knows your style the best?

3 Which style has most difficulty developing MT&R?

4 Which style has the least difficulty developing MT&R?

-Conversation 7-

Review Questions

1 Which style has one year of experience repeated twenty times, rather than twenty years of experience?

2 Which political parties try to stop change?

3 Which religions try to stop change?

4 Who has succeeded in stopping change sustainably in the history of mankind?

5 There is no textbook leader, one who performs all **(PAEI)** roles well. Is this true or false?

6 Why does being "open-minded" mean having respect?

7 Does respect mean how you handle a discussion, without raising your voice or being offensive?

8 Is it open-mindedness that causes respect, or is it respect that causes you to be open-minded?

9 Define respect. How different is it from honoring someone? Use **(PAEI)** code in your explanation.

10 What does self-respect mean?

11 Is American culture based on mutual respect? How is it nourished? Compare it to a European country's culture. Compare it to that of a developing country in trouble.

Application Questions

1 How would you rejuvenate a Deadwood who was previously an **(E)** type?

2 How would you rejuvenate a Deadwood who was previously the **(I)** type?

3 Does having all **(PAEI)** roles performed well mean that an organization is managed well? What else do you need, if anything, to say that and organization is well managed?

4 "A **(PAEI)** organization is healthy." Discuss whether this is necessarily true.

5 To be healthy you need a system in which all **(PAEI)** roles are fulfilled. What else do you need?

6 Diversity of cultures and/or styles can be a blessing or a curse. When will it be a blessing and when a curse?

7 "Do not work on your weaknesses. Complement yourself instead." Do you agree with this statement?

8 What is the **(PAEI)** style of your partner, spouse, or significant other?

9 Are you two complementary? Do you respect each other?

Development Questions

1 Which type of Deadwood is the most difficult to rejuvenate: that which was previously was **(P)**, **(A)**, **(E)**, or **(I)**?

2 Are there Deadwoods who are “dead” not because of change but for other reasons? What are they? How would you rejuvenate them?

3 Are there situations where it is not prudent to rejuvenate Deadwood?

4 In which stage of the lifecycle would you find more Deadwood as a percentage of total employees: in Bureaucracy or in Go-Go?

5 What are the collateral effects of deregulating an industry?

6 React to this statement: "We are getting older younger." What does it mean? When would it be true?

7 If there is no (PAEI) individual who excels in all the roles, and if a **(PAEI)** organization is a healthy organization, does it mean then that there is no such thing as a perfectly healthy organization?

8 A human body is a complementary system. Diseases develop when the relationship get sour. Do you agree? Discuss, giving examples.

9 How do you keep a system healthy? What does it mean for a system to be healthy?

10 Are eating right, exercising, and sleeping enough to keep healthy? Use **(PAEI)** code to analyze your answer.

11 "Best marry a girl from your neighborhood," a mother says to her son. That negates diversity, right? Should a person marry from a different culture?

12 In the West, and in developed countries, we are going through a new type of revolution: from industrial to postindustrial society, from villages to metropolitan macro cities, from national companies to multinational companies. What are the conflicts that those changes cause, and which are the utopian theories that are emerging to deal with those conflicts?

13 Is modern democracy, especially in the USA as of 2016, based on mutual respect or not? What signs do you have to support your argument?

14 Where did the socialist, and Communist, ideology go wrong?

15 Where is the capitalist, market economy theory going wrong and why?

16 What should the third way, not socialism nor capitalism, be?

17 Is dictatorship based on mutual respect? Does your answer explain why dictatorships eventually make disastrous decisions for a country?

18 Explain why a sustainable democracy should be all encompassing, from how a family is run, to how companies are run, and how a country is run.

19 Can you have political democracy in a culture that discriminates against women? One that abuses children? Why or why not?

20 Discuss how the human organism is comprised of complementary subsystems. What does mutual respect mean physiologically?

-Conversation 8-

Review Questions

1 "If you start labeling people, your tendency will be to change the people rather than changing the environment that causes their behavior." Discuss and give examples from your experience where this is true or not true.

2 What are the four imperatives of decision making? Or should they be the imperatives of decision *taking* or *accepting*?

3 Why are they "imperatives?"

4 Is the **(E)** imperative *by when*, or just *when*? Why?

5 What does it mean a decision "must be bound"? Give an example.

6 How easy or difficult is it to bind a decision?

7 Why do we say: "Do not only expect, inspect?"

8 The book says, "the right to make certain decisions." Is the book right or wrong?

9 In a bureaucracy who can say yes to strategic change?

10 "The greater the rate of change, the greater the level of uncertainty, which, in turn, requires more influence." Defend this argument or criticize it.

11 "The greater the uncertainty, the better the teamwork will have to be, or in a chronically changing situation bureaucracy will mushroom." Defend this argument or criticize it.

12 What is the difference between responsibility and accountability?

13 Why does capi equal control?

Application Questions

1 Discuss a case where a decision did not have the four imperatives well defined. What happened?

2 Politicians spend or should spend time studying the style of their opponents to predict decisions they will make. Can you diagnose why Barack Obama and Benjamin Netanyahu have a dislike for each other?

3 “Good decisions are based on good judgment. Good judgment is derived from bad experiences.” Discuss this statement in light of the instruction to bind decisions.

4 “Intelligent people know how to get out of a hole. Wise people know how not to fall into the hole.” Discuss using the material in this conversation.

5 “Intelligent people learn from experience Wise people learn from experience of others.” Discuss using the material learned in this conversation.

6 Discuss the following quote from Margaret Mead: "You do not have to be a horse to be a veterinarian."

7 "There is really no such thing as a good decision, it's only a good decision for the time being." Provide an example from your personal experience why this is true or not.

8 Discuss an experience you have had where the authority to say yes has not been delegated but the right to say no has been.

9 "Assign tasks to those who have authority to deal with it, not those who are responsible for it." Explain why this is right or wrong.

10 Discuss an experience you have had or know of where a task was assigned to a person who was held responsible but who had no authority. Who had authority but did not feel responsible? What happened?

11 In your company, or one where you have worked, what percentage of responsibility do people take and what percentage is given but not taken? What about authority? Where is this organization on the lifecycle?

12 Discuss an example when you sacrificed efficiency for effectiveness, and vice versa.

13 Discuss a situation when you got things done without having authority to order implementation but used power instead.

14 Discuss a situation in which you used influence to get implementation. Why is it a punishment to overpromise and underdeliver?

15 Can you think of an example of an army that lost a war because their leaders were leading from behind?

16 Discuss a situation in which you have authority without power.

17 Discuss a situation in which you had power without authority.

18 Discuss a situation in which you had authority with influence.

19 Present a situation in which you had capi.

20 Present a situation in which someone has indirect power.

Challenge Questions

1 Why are authority, power, and influence defined in the book as sources of "managerial energy?"

2 Organizational therapy is to heal an organization. To heal means to make it whole, to integrate. Discuss at least six ways in which Adizes Methodology integrates organizations.

3 Authority should not be equal to responsibility. Discuss why this is correct, and what the repercussions are for trust and respect.

4 "Being alive means not being fully in control." Do you accept this as a

guideline for living a healthy life? What are the repercussions of accepting this dictum?

5 Discuss how control grows: The more you control the more you need to control.

6 In situations of higher uncertainty should you have more or less control?

7 Discuss how to prevent a government agency from becoming too bureaucratic.

8 Why is it true that the less you expect the happier you will be? Use the tools provided in this conversation to explain your answer.

9 Using the concepts from this chapter, discuss why being in love can be painful.

10 Discuss why the more modern the society the less empowered people feel.

-Conversation 9-

Review Questions

1 Draw an Adizesgram—a diagram of the square of your responsibility and how much authority, power, and influence, or any combination of authorance you have over it. Share it with someone else and explain it with examples.

2 Present a case from your experience or the literature in which power without authority backfired.

3 Present a case from your experience or the literature in which indirect power was used. What happened?

4 Present a case from your experience or the literature in which a person had full capi. Did he or she lose it eventually? Why?

5 Define managerial effectiveness. How is it different from organizational effectiveness?

6 Define managerial efficiency. How is it different from organizational efficiency?

7 What does it mean that someone has influence over you? How? What is the source of their influence? Is it enough that they know how to speak convincingly?

8 What does it mean that someone has power over you? How?

Application Questions

1 How should you seek the cooperation of people whose influence you need?

2 How should you seek the cooperation of people who have power over you?

3 How should you seek the cooperation of people who have authority over you with

you having no influence nor power? With influence and/or power?

4 Present a case from your experience or the literature in which a problem was presented and ignored by the person who was aware of it because he or she did not consider it his or her responsibility. What happened?

5 Present a case in which a leader only used authority with no power and no influence. What happened?

6 Present a case in which a pre-problem was handled as if it were a problem. What happened?

7 Present a case in which a problem was handled as if it were a pre-problem. What happened?

8 Firing people is expensive. Why? Not firing people is also expensive. How? What should you do?

9 Present a case in which you had a pre-pre-problem. How did it turn out? What did you do right? What did you do wrong?

10 Present a case in which a problem was an opportunity in disguise.

11 Present a case in which an opportunity was a problem in disguise.

12 Present a case in which you thought a person said yes but it was actually maybe in disguise. What was that person's style?

13 Present a case in which a person said no but you understood it to mean maybe. What was your style and what was the style of the other person? Could it have been not a style difference but a cultural difference?

Challenge Questions

1 "A leader is a person who is not responsible for anything and is responsible for everything." Do you agree or disagree? Explain.

2 "You can delegate responsibility but that does not absolve you from having it." Defend or criticize this statement.

3 In a well-functioning democracy, every citizen should feel responsible for what is happening in the country. What needs to happen for this to be true? What are the barriers in modern society for this to happen?

4 Is democracy, as we know it, in danger? Why or why not?

5 Do you have capi if you have authority and power but no influence?

6 What does it mean not to have influence? Can you get things done with just authority and power with no influence? How good will your decision be? How well will your solution to the problem work?

7 Explain why management and labor need to cooperate. Use the concepts presented in this conversation.

8 "We should have capitalism in the marketplace and socialism in the company." Explain what this means. How will it work? Do you agree with the statement? Why or why not?

9 What would you call a situation that is your responsibility, but all you have is power, with no authority or influence? Explain this situation.

10 What should you do when you have only power for what you are responsible?

11 "Treat others as you want to be treated. "Is this the right prescription for communication? Why or why not?

12 If you have capi you do not need to use influence; you can just decide, use authority and power, and it will be enough. Do you agree? Where is the component of time pressure here? How does it impact your strategy?

-Conversation 10-

Review Questions

1 Summarize the essence of what have you learned so far in no more than ten sentences.

2 What is needed to make an organization healthy?

3 Is having all the **(PAEI)** roles enough to for an organization to be effective and efficient in the short and long term?

4 What is the difference between having a healthy decision and a healthy organization?

5 "The purpose of management, leadership, government, or parenting is to see that the **(PAEI)** roles are performed, that the system is healthy." Do you agree?

6 How would you measure or validate commitment?

7 "There must be mutual trust that, in the long term, things will work out and interests will be equally satisfied." Do you agree? Discuss.

8 "The more mutual trust and respect there is the easier it is to lead change." Do you agree?

9 What must come first: trust or respect? Why?

10 Do respect and trust have to be mutual? Why? Give examples to support your conclusion.

11 Mutual trust and respect are not stable. What erodes them?

12 What do you need to do to sustain a culture of mutual trust and respect?

13 What are the four factors that produce MT&R?

14 Are these four factors in any way related to **(PAEI)**?

15 What kind of leaders project MT&R?

16 How and why do common vision and values nourish MT&R?

Application Questions

1 Think of a situation in which you could not get to common interests because you could not identify a higher purpose.

2 Analyze any book on management or leadership. Is it a collage of many people or a description of one person? If it was describing one person, did that person have weaknesses?

3 Describe a situation from your experience or the literature in which change caused common interests to disband.

4 Present a case from your experience or the literature in which leadership used its authority and power for self-interest at the expense of the organization they were leading.

5 Present a case in which those in power used their power for self-interest only.

6 Present a case in which those with influence used it for self-interest only.

7 "First, accept reality. Only when you accept that there is conflict can you harness it." Do you agree or disagree?

Present a case to support your conclusion.

8 "There is no love without mutual trust and respect." Do you agree? Do you have an example of this statement being true or false?

9 Can you love someone you do not trust? Can you love someone you do not respect?

10 "Love makes you look younger; hate makes you look older." Discuss why this is true or false. Give examples.

11 How can the decision-making process nourish mutual trust? What about mutual respect?

12 How should an organizational structure nourish trust? Respect?

13 Do all organizational development programs you know develop mutual trust and respect? Do you have any experience where this is not true? Describe them.

14 Do you have an example in which MT&R was exploited rather than nourished? Describe and analyze it.

15 Describe from experience or literature a case in which attempts to develop mutual trust and respect failed because the right development sequence was not being followed.

Challenge Questions

1 "Implementation is always faster if propelled by integrated self-interests." Do you agree?

2 Can you have integrating interests be a higher purpose without mutual trust?

3 Can there be mutual trust without mutual commitment?

4 Can there be mutual commitment without higher purpose? Without a long-term goal?

5 How would you test trust? Should you test it?

6 To be healthy is it enough to be effective and efficient in the short and long term?

-Conversation 11-

Review Questions

Identify the style code characterized by each statement below.

1. He likes subordinates to emulate his own ways of accomplishing tasks.

2. She knows most of the standard operating procedures by heart.

3. He changes direction without warning.

4. She often says if she can do it, you should be able to do it too.

5 He tries to figure out which way the political wind is blowing within the organization, and then he tries to follow in that direction.

6 He spreads himself too thin.

7 She spreads others too thin.

8 He manages largely by writing directives.

9 She believes that we should not worry too much about long-term planning. She says if we don't achieve results today there might be no tomorrow.

10 He thinks that anyone who can't do a job is an academician.

11 The best thing to do is avoid her because she always has a new job for you to do in spite of the fact that you are already occupied.

12 His main concern is always to achieve a consensus within the organization.

13 She has little sense of what people are capable of accomplishing.

14 He becomes very excited about his own ideas.

15 She prefers to get results working alone.

16 He considers departmental tasks his own personal responsibility.

17 She does not care about achieving anything beyond controlling the organization's behavior.

18 He delegates new responsibilities and duties before the old ones have been accomplished.

19 She always has many reasons at hand to show why changes should not be made.

20 He expects that success should have been achieved already.

21 She likes to see the organization kept busy, regardless of the results it is producing.

22 He tries to accomplish tasks by himself.

23 If there is a power struggle going on among members of the organization, she will not intervene until it is already resolved one way or the other.

24 His subordinates try to look busy in order not to receive additional tasks.

25 She thinks that no one can do things as well as she can.

26 He takes risks.

27 She cares more about how things are done than about what is being done.

28 He becomes upset when tasks are not accomplished even though he had given his subordinates the impression that those tasks had been abandoned.

29 She relies on expeditors, i.e., assistants who do not have a permanent role but who carry out special assignments that she gives them.

30 His subordinates accept assignments but do not carry them out because they are not sure if he really means what he is asking them to do.

31 Cliques and special interest groups flourish under her management.

32 He changes his mind frequently.

33 She does not delegate enough.

34 He does not follow up on assignments on a regular basis.

For the following questions, identify which style would say the provided quote. It may be more than one letter, like (PA) for example.

1 "Between two living beings, harmony is never given. It has to be worked on again and again." – advertising for the World Equestrian Games, Jerez

2 "I like it, I do it. That is my code." – Alain Delon

3 "Be not afraid of going slowly; be only afraid of standing still." – Chinese proverb

4 "*Per ardua ad astra*." ("By striving we reach the stars.") – Royal Air Force motto

5 "It is far easier to begin a task than to finish it." – Titus Maccius Plautus

6 "If it isn't happening, make it happen." – David Hemmings

7 "All that I can, I will." – French saying

8 "There is no penalty for overachievement." – George William Miller

9 "The only people who never fail are those who never try." – Ilka Chase

10 "Act as if it were impossible to fail." – Dorothea Brande

11 "Man needs difficulties; they are necessary for health." – Carl Jung

12 "The road to success is always under construction." – Arnold Palmer

13 "If you are going to be thinking anyway, you might as well think big." – Donald Trump

14 "No one knows what is in him until he tries, and many would never try if they were not forced to." – Basil W. Maturin

15 "Just keep going. Everybody gets better if they keep at it." – Ted Williams

16 "You see things and you say, 'Why?' But I dream things that never were;

and I say, 'Why not?'" – George Bernard Shaw

17 "Winning is living. Every time you win, you're reborn. When you lose, you die a little." – George Allen

18 "Sweat is the cologne of accomplishment." – Heywood Hale Brown

19 "When you reach the top that is when the climb begins." – Michael Caine

20 "We strain hardest for things which are almost but not quite within our reach." – Frederick W. Faber

21 "The only place where success comes before work is in the dictionary." – Vidal Sassoon

22 "It ain't over 'til it's over." – Yogi Berra

23 "Just get out there and do what you've got to do." – unattributed

Application Questions

1 Diagnose the styles of the people you are working with. Describe a situation where you misread their style and how it created a conflict of styles and miscommunication.

2 How do **(P)**s plan?

3 How do **(E)**s plan?

4 How do **(A)**s plan?

5 How do **(I)**s plan?

6 Which style might say something like, "All I remember is tomorrow?"

7 Which style usually has difficulty keeping eye contact in a conversation?

8 Which style is the best at maintaining eye contact in a conversation?

9 Which style might tell you, "Speak slowly so I can understand you fast?"

10 Describe a situation in which you had to change your style in order to complement the person you were talking to. (For instance, you were talking to a bigger **(E)** than you are, so you naturally started to act like an **(A)**.)

11 Describe a situation where when you were in a back-up behavior. What happened?

Challenge Questions

1 Are styles driven physiologically?

2 How difficult or easy is it to change a style?

3 Compare the Myer Briggs personality styles to the **(PAEI)** styles.

-Conversation 12-

Review Questions

1 Describe a case from your experience or from history in which an **(E)** stuck to his dream, does what he *wants* and believes what he wants *should* be, ignoring the *is*, and went bankrupt.

2 Describe a situation in which you ignored the *is* and acted based on *want* only, translating the *should* into *want* language. What happened?

3 All change should start with *is*. But doesn't accepting what *is* stop you from instigating change? Discuss.

4 Describe a situation from literature or personal experience in which there was so much change that the end result was that nothing really changed.

-Conversation 13-

Review Questions

1 What destroys a marriage? Conflicts?

2 What is the dominant style of your partner or spouse?

3 What is your dominant style?

4 How do you two handle your conflicts?

5 Think of someone you do not want to work with anymore? What was the conflict you two had? How was it handled?

6 What signs indicate whether you respect someone or not?

7 What signs show you whether you trust someone or not?

8 Define a symbiotic relationship.

9 Define a synergetic relationship.

10 Define symbergetic behavior.

11 Is “capitalism with conscience” symbergetic?

12 Is participative management in decision making symbergetic?

13 Are ESOP plans symbergetic?

14 What is your personal external integration goal?

15 What does it mean to have internal integration in personal life?

16 Give an example of unattended change being destructive by its nature.

17 What are the characteristics of good leaders?

18 Compare the characteristics of good leaders as defined by Adizes to other theories of leadership.

Application Questions

1 Think of someone who has inherited lots of money but cannot be successful in life because of low self MT&R. How did that happen?

2 How can your mind, body, emotions, and spirit be in conflict? Give an example.

3 How do you develop self-trust and self-respect? What does it mean?

4 How much of the education system in your country is dedicated to teaching students to know and how much of it is focused on teaching them to be?

5 How should education focus on "to be?" What would you do to make that happen?

6 How much internal disintegration exists in the company you work for? What is causing it?

7 How much internal disintegration is there is in your country? What is causing it?

8 Is it true that political and economic stability are sources of a country's success? Give examples.

9 Give example of a country with vast natural resources but no economic or and political stability. What is happening in that country?

10 "The tragedy of colonialism is not what the colonists took out of the colonies, but the culture and system they left behind or reinforced." Give an example that illustrates this statement and discuss it.

11 "What you have is the result of who you are, while who you are is not the result of what you have." Give an example to illustrate this point.

12 Give an example in which a great opportunity in the marketplace was missed or mishandled due to a bad internal environment.

13 "Think Yiddish, act British." Do you know of anyone who acts this way? Describe his or her behavior.

14 Describe a situation where the battle was won but the war was lost, that is, the person won the argument, but the relationship ended. Why?

Challenge Questions

1 Russia has never had a democratic regime—it has always been some kind of dictatorship. Are the people there used to dictatorship? Would they appreciate a democratic leader? Would they respect and trust someone who is not dictatorial?

2 Do you agree that it is easier to communicate with people in developing countries than people in developed countries? Why or why not?

3 "A way to know yourself is by paying attention to what you do to others." Do you pay attention to this? Why or why

not? What could be a good routine to force you to pay attention to the effect of your style on others?

4 "The road to heaven is through hell." Give some examples to illustrate this idea.

5 Why do teenagers sleep a lot? Can you explain it using Adizes Methodology?

6 Why is a diamond the strongest stone?

7 Why is the diamond the symbol of love?

8 If we are weak inside, an outside opportunity looks like a problem. If we are strong inside an outside problem looks like an opportunity. Give examples of these points.

9 Do you agree with the diagnosis made in the book about MT&R and the Jewish people? What about the book's diagnosis of Israel?

10 "There will be no peace in the Middle East until MT&R is established." What is causing breakdown of trust and respect on both sides? Is there hope for peace in the Middle East?

11 Who has a better chance of leading the world in the future: China, India, Brazil, the US, or Europe? Why? Use the tools provided by Adizes to explain.

12 "There can be no tolerance of systems that renounce tolerance." How does this idea apply to the terror state the world is in the beginning of the twenty-first century?

13 What should the **(PAEI)** sequence for treatment of a developing country after emancipation from colonialism be? Do you have an example in which the sequence was wrong? One where it was right?

-Conversation 14-

Review Questions

1 How do you define respect?

2 "In order to make effective decisions, a complementary team is necessary." Do you agree? Why or why not?

3 What are the various sources of conflict in an organization? How does Adizes attempt to remove them?

4 Why is open communication necessary for mutual trust and respect?

Application Questions

1 Identify the unspoken rules that govern your marriage or another relationship. If you have children, identify the unspoken rules that govern how you parent.

2 Describe a situation in which you broke some rules you did not know existed and were embarrassed.

3 "I do not care whether you trust and respect me or not. Act as if you do." Does this philosophy make sense? Why or why not?

4 Is there a danger that you will be taken if you trust a person without that person first proving he or she is trustworthy?

5 Describe a situation in which a disastrous decision was made in a prolonged meeting.

6 How much pain can you take in meetings?

7 Is there a leader you admire? How does that person handle conflicts?

8 Think of a conversation that, in trying to make it short, you made very long. Describe a conversation in which you took the long route and it ended fast.

Challenge Questions

1 Why is transparency necessary for democracy?

2 When there is no transparency, what happens to an organization? To a country? To a marriage?

-Conversation 15-

Review Questions

1 What are the eleven phases of Adizes organizational transformation?

i. ______

ii. ______

iii. ______

iv. ______

v. ______

vi. ______

vii. ______

viii. ______

ix. ______

x. ______

xi. ______

xii. ______

2 Why is strategic planning in phase IX?

______

______

______

3 Why is mission definition in phase IV?

4 Why is the capability to lead upwards important?

5 Should we assign problems by responsibility or by authority? Why?

Application Questions

1 Compare the Adizes organizational transformation program to another consulting methodology you know.

2 How is Adizes' mission definition different from how missions are usually defined?

www.ingramcontent.com/pod-product-compliance
Lightning Source LLC
Chambersburg PA
CBHW060040030426
42334CB00019B/2422

* 9 7 8 0 9 7 9 1 6 3 8 6 9 *